GOING FAR

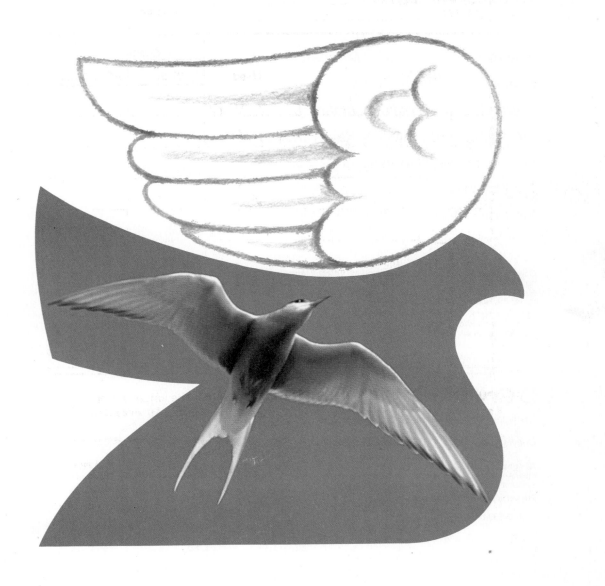

CONSULTANTS

Mildred Bailey	**Teresa Flores**	**Nancy Mayeda**
Rose Barragan	**Charles Hacker**	**Kenneth Smith**
Barbara Burke	**P.J. Hutchins**	**Lydia Stack**
Barbara B. Cramer	**George Jurata**	**Mary Wigner**
Wilma J. Farmer		

Executive Editor: *Sandra Maccarone*

Senior Editor: *Ronne Kaufman*

Design Director: *Leslie Bauman*

Assistant Design Director: *Kay Wanous*

Designer: *Lillie Caporlingua*

Production Director: *Barbara Arkin*

Production Manager: *Trudy Pisciotti*

Cover, Front Matter, Photo Essay designed by: *Thomas Vroman Associates, Inc.* Illustrators: Tony Rao, pp. 8-13; Renee Daily, pp. 14-20; Sal Murdocca, pp. 21-28; Jerry Smath, pp. 29-37; Joy Friedman, pp. 38-42; Jerry Smath, pp. 43-50; Susan Lexa, pp. 51-57; Nancy Schill, pp. 58-64; Tony Rao, pp. 65-70; Sue Parnell, pp. 71-77; Barbara McClintock, pp. 78-82; Tien Ho, pp. 83-89; Robbie Stillerman, pp. 90-96.

Photo Credits: K. W. Fink, Ardea Photographics, cover and p. 1; Mike Mazzaschi, Stock Boston, p. 3; Jay Dorin, p. 4; Susan Johns, Rapho/Photo Researchers, p. 5; Al Kaplan, D.P.I., p. 6; Douglas Mesney, Leo de Wys, p. 7 (left); NASA, p. 7 (right); Michael Heran, pp. 38-42.

D.C. HEATH AND COMPANY

Lexington, Massachusetts/Toronto, Ontario

ISBN 0-669-04964-6

3   5   7   9   11   13   14   12   10   8   6   4   2

Contents

Let's Go

7

A Fish Is a Fish

A fish is a fish,
And a fish I will be!
I will not go with you.
I wish to be me.

So why come to me?
Why come with a net?
I will not go with you.
I will not be a pet.

I do what I wish.
And I WISH a lot.
I DO NOT wish to be
A fish in a pot.

I come and I go.
And I do what I wish.
I will not go and be
A fish in a dish!

11

Who can you get
To go in the net?
Who will it be?
Not me, you can bet!

Not me in a net!
Not me in a dish!
Not me in a pot!
I do what I wish!

Candy

"Look at Mop," said Dan.

"He wants some candy," said Ruth.
"May he have some?"

"No," said Dan.
"Candy is not good for dogs!
Get down, Mop.
You are in the way.
Go out and play!"

15

"Please, Dan," said Ruth.
"Please let Mop have some candy."

"No, Ruth," said Dan.
"The candy is not good for Mop."

"Mop, candy is not good for you,"
said Ruth.
"Come out and play.
You and I are in the way."

Dan said, "Come in, Ruth.
Come in.
You may have some candy.
And Mop, you may not."

"Not so good, is it?" said Ruth.

"No, it is NOT!" said Dan.
"It is not good for Mop.
It is not good for you and me."

Ruth said, "Can we go out and play?"

Let Me Out!

"Look at that!"
said the hen.
"I will sit on it.
I will sit and sit."

21

So the hen sat and sat.

"Let me out!" it said.
"Please let me out!"

"What?" said the hen.
"Who said that?"

23

"Me," it said.
"Please let me out!"

"Come on out,"
said the hen.

24

"Out I come!" it said.
"I am out.
No, I am not out.
I am IN.
Why am I in a pen?"

"The dog,"
said the hen.

"What is a dog?"
it said to the hen.

27

"HELP! HELP!
Let me in!
Let me in!" it said.

The Thing

Rosa met a fish.

"Who are you?"
she said.
"Are you a girl?"

"Yes," said the fish.
"I am Patty."

Then Patty and Rosa met a hen.

"Who are you?" said Patty.

"Are you a boy?" said Rosa.
"Are you Ben?"

"No," said the hen.
"I am not Ben.
I am Tony."

Then Rosa and Patty and Tony met a Thing.

"Who are you?" Rosa said to the Thing.

"Beep! Beep!" said the Thing.
"I can hop and I can sing.
When I wish, I can ring."

"You ARE Ben!" said Tony.

"Beep! Beep!" said the Thing.
"I can ring and I can hop.
When I wish, I can stop."

"Come on, Ben," said Tony.
"It is YOU!"

"No, I am Ben," said the dog.
"That Thing is NOT me."

"Then who are YOU?"
Rosa said to the Thing.

"Beep! Beep!" said the Thing.
"I can sing and I can play.
But who I am, I can not say."

"Come on," said Patty.
"Who ARE you?"

"Who am I?" said the Thing.
"Who I am, I can not say.
I have to go, but you can play."

Good Try

It is a good day.
Jerry, Andy, and Robin play ball.
Jerry gets it.
Robin gets it.
Then Andy gets it.

"I want to get the ball in," said Jerry.
"Do you want to try, Andy?"

"I am small," said Andy.
"But I will try."

"Will you play with us?" said Jerry.

"I will play," said Robin.

"Look at Robin," said Andy.
"She got the ball all the way up!"

"And she got the ball in!" said Jerry.

"I want to try," said Andy.

"And I want to try," said Jerry.

40

"Look at Andy!
Look at that ball!
What a good try!"
said Robin.

"Look at Jerry!
Look at that ball!
What a good try!"
said Andy.

"Look at us," said Andy.
"We got the ball up.
But we can not get it in yet."

"One day you will," said Robin.

42

The Three Little Pigs

45

47

50

Suzy Calls

"The Reds are going to play the Tops. The Reds want you to play," said Jimmy. "Will you play with us, Suzy?"

"No, I can not," said Suzy. "The Reds AND the Tops want me. So I am going to call the plays."

51

"Why are you calling the plays?"
said Jimmy.
"You can help us win.
Why not play with us?"

"No, I will call the balls," said Suzy.
"I will call the hits.
I will call the outs."

Suzy was calling the plays.
Then Jimmy was up.

"Ball one," said Suzy.
"Ball two."

Then Jimmy hit the ball.
It was a good hit!

The Reds said,
"Go all the way, Jimmy!
Help us win!"

But Bobby got the ball!
Was Jimmy out?

Jimmy was looking at Suzy.
"What do you say, Suzy?" he said.

"You are out," said Suzy.

"You are calling the plays,"
said Jimmy.

"Yes," said Suzy.
"You are out.
But that was SOME hit!"

Who Fed the Dog?

"OK, boys," said Maria.
"Up to bed!"

"Do we have to?" said Mike.

"Yes," said Maria.
"You have to go to bed."

"May the dog come to bed
with us?" said Jerry.

"No," said Maria.
"She may not go to bed with you."

"OK," said the boys.

60

"By the way," said Maria.
"Is the dog out?
Is she OK?"

"Yes, she is," said Mike.
"She is out in the shed."

"She is OK," said Jerry.
"It is my day.
So I fed her."

"YOU?" said Mike.
"YOU fed her?
But it is MY day!
I fed her!"

"You fed the dog, Jerry?"
said Maria.
"You fed her, Mike?
I fed her!
We ALL fed the dog!"

"Is she OK?" said the boys.

"Go out to the shed and get her,"
said Maria.

"Is she OK?" said Maria.

"Yes, but she can not sit up!"
said Jerry.

"She will go to bed with us,"
said Mike.

"Why?" said Maria.

"She will not fit in the shed!"
said the boys.

64

Ten Pins Down

"May we play?" say the boys.
"What do we have to do?"

"You have to get the pins down,"
say the men.

"OK," say the boys.
"May we try?"

"You can try," say the men.
"Try to get ALL the pins down.
Get ten pins down.
Then you will win."

"We will try," say the boys.
"We can do it!
Yes, we can.
We can get ten pins down."

Bobby gets a ball.
And Carlos gets a ball.

"What are you going to do?
You can not do that!
STOP!" say the men.

But the boys do it!

The boys hit the pins.
Some pins fall down.
Then all the pins fall down.

"We win! We win!" say the boys.
"We got ten pins down."

"You got all the pins," say the men.
"That is NOT the way we play.
But it is OK."

Singing in a Can

"Come on, Pig," said Cat.
"Get in the can with me.
We are going to sing.
We are going to sing in the can."

"OK," said Pig.
Pig got in the can.

"May I come in?" said Dog.
"I want to sing in the can with you."

"Come in," said Cat.

"May I come in?" said Rabbit.

"Yes," said Cat.
"Get in!"

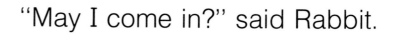

Cat said, "All of you may come.
All of you may get in the can.
Then we will sing.
We will all sing in the can."

One was singing in the can.
Two were singing in the can.
Then all were singing in the can.

But Skunk was not singing in the can.
He was looking for Rabbit.

RABBIT

"Come out! Come out!"
said Skunk.

"What hit us?" said Rabbit.

"Stop it!" said Cat.
"Stop it, Skunk!"

Pig said, "Do not hit the can.
We were singing in the can.
Come sing with us!"

"No! No!
That may be singing to you,"
said Skunk.
"But that is NOT singing to me!"

Who Is Carl?

"Please, may I play with Carl?"
said Jenny.

"Yes," said Robin.
"You may play with my cat."

"Why is Carl so fat?
Was he fat when you got him?"
said Jenny.

78

"No," said Robin.
"We got him at the pet shop.
Then he was not fat."

"I bet you have fed that cat a lot,"
said Jenny.

"No, not a lot," said Robin.
"He gets one can of fish a day."

"I wish Carl were my cat," said Jenny.

"You may play with him," said Robin.
"Come by when you want to play."

"OK, I will," said Jenny.
"I have to go.
But I will come and play with Carl a lot."

80

One day, Jenny said, "May I pet Carl?"

"No, you may not pet him," said Robin.
"You may not play with him."

"Why not?" said Jenny.

"I do not have Carl," said Robin.

81

"I have CARLA!"

82

The Good Day

Was it a good day?
It WAS a good day.
But it was not ALL good.

Mike fed my fish.
That was good.
But he fed him candy.
That was NOT so good.

Ruth let me have her ring.
That was good.
But it was small for me.
That was NOT so good.

I was playing ball.
That was good.
But the ball hit a dish.
That was NOT so good.

Two of us sat in my shed.
That was good.
One of us got wet.
That was NOT so good.

I met a girl who was falling down.
That was NOT so good.

"Please let me help you up," I said.
That was good.

"You are good to me," she said.
And she let me have one of her pets.

All in all, I have to say,
"It WAS a good day!"

To Win a Fish

"I wish, I wish,
to have a pet fish," said Jimmy.

"You can get one at the pet shop,"
said Jenny.

"I will look in my pig," said Jimmy.

"No, ten will not do it.
That will not get me a fish."
said Jimmy.

"Get the pig and come with me,"
said Jenny.

"You can WIN a fish.
Come and try," said Jenny.

"That one looks good.
I will try to play Ring the Thing,"
said Jimmy.

"Not yet. Try that one,"
said Jenny.
"Try to get the ball in the net."

"I will do it.
I will not stop," said Jimmy.

"You have to try and try," said Jenny.

"I will try Hit the Pins. I may be good at that," said Jimmy.

"I have one to go.
I DO want to win a fish.
I will play Wet the Skunk,"
said Jimmy.

"You can do it!"
said Jenny.

"You hit the skunk!" said Dan.
"You can win a fish in a dish.
You can win a candy rabbit.
Do you want a small hen?"

"I wish, I wish,
to have a pet fish," said Jimmy.